YOUTUI

SCRIPTING FOR SUCCESS

TIPS AND STRATEGIES FOR CRAFTING ENGAGING AND EFFECTIVE VIDEOS

BENJAMIN WILLIAMS

YOUTUBE SCRIPTING FOR SUCCESS

Tips and Strategies for Crafting Engaging and Effective Videos

Benjamin Williams

YouTube Scripting for Success:
Tips and Strategies for Crafting Engaging and Effective Videos

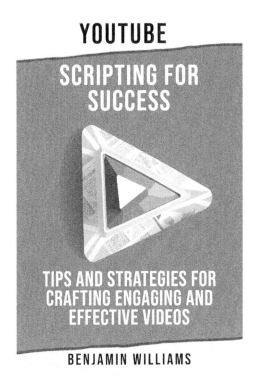

INTRODUCTION

L ooking to enhance your YouTube channel? Do you want to know how to write a script that will draw viewers in and make your videos popular? Look nowhere else! This engaging and (hopefully) informative second part of the *YouTube Success in 2023 series* delves into the world of YouTube scripting. My goal is to help you with the fundamental aspects of the scripting process. The help will range from developing concepts that will keep viewers returning to your channel to writing and producing videos that will leave them wanting more; eventually building and expanding an audience that will cause your channel to go viral.

Throughout this guide I want to show you how to write a script that will make your ideas come to life and set your videos apart from the competition. I want to show you how to develop an engaging story that will captivate your audience and compel them to keep watching by teaching you how to brainstorm, outline, research, and write like a YouTube professional.

Another aspect I want to cover is more personal. Sure, I could provide you with all the technical information in the world, but without the confidence to properly execute your script, it's worthless. This is why I also want to demonstrate how to write and deliver your script in an engaging and self-assured manner, utilizing body language and colloquialisms to inject humor and personality into your content, allowing you to stand out and building a successful brand *(whatever that may be for you!)*.

Let's Jump In!

CHAPTER 1: THE FUNDAMENTALS

Building a solid base.

A good YouTube script should begin with a brief introduction that clearly states the topic or theme of the video. This introduction should be engaging and captivating, drawing the viewer in and setting the stage for the rest of the video. It should also provide a brief overview of the key points or ideas that will be covered in the video, giving the viewer a sense of what to expect.

The main body of the script should then provide a detailed outline of the key points or ideas that will be covered in the video. This outline should be organized in a logical and clear manner, with each point or idea building on the previous one. It should also be concise and to-the-point, avoiding unnecessary details or tangents.

In addition to the written content of the script, it should also include any dialogue or narration that will be used in the video. This dialogue should be well-written and engaging, and should be delivered in a clear and natural-sounding way. It should also be written in a conversational, colloquial style that is relatable to the intended audience.

Though not vital, I would suggest that the script should also include any visual elements or graphics that will be included in the video. These elements should be carefully planned and integrated into the script, ensuring that they enhance the overall message and story of the video.

I would also argue that they should also be visually appealing and engaging, helping to keep the viewer's attention throughout the video. To better understand the best graphics to use without, you will need to undertake extensive *research.*

Research Your Topic

Conducting thorough and effective research is a fundamental aspect of creating a YouTube script. To ensure that your research is as useful as possible, I have found that it's helpful to follow a structured approach. Though I do tend to break this now, they do always say master the rules first so you can break them later.

The first step is to determine the main goal or purpose of your research. What do you hope to learn or accomplish through your research? This will help you focus your efforts and ensure that your research is relevant and useful.

The second is to identify the key questions or issues that you want to explore through your research. What specific information or insights are you looking for?

After that, develop a plan or strategy for conducting your research. This might involve identifying relevant sources of information such as books, articles, websites, or experts, and determining how you will access and evaluate this information. As you conduct your research, take careful and detailed notes on the information you find. Make sure to include the source of each piece of information, as well as any relevant quotes or statistics.

As you gather and organize your information, look for patterns, trends, or themes that emerge. What insights or conclusions can you draw from the information you have collected?

Remember, review and evaluate your research to ensure that it is accurate, relevant, and complete. Have you addressed all of the key questions or issues that you identified at the beginning of your research? Are there any gaps or inconsistencies in your information?

You can follow these steps or create your own, but I have always found it beneficial to follow a systematic and organized approach. I argue that this allows for better research a topic and the ability to gain valuable insights and knowledge, ultimately creating a more informed and effective YouTube script.

Brainstorming Tips

Brainstorming a YouTube script can be a challenging but crucial step in the process of creating a successful video. How you physically brainstorm is up to you, be it at a cafe with a notepad, or at home on a whiteboard. I know I have mentioned this before but I have found adhesive whiteboard strips which can be stuck to glass invaluable during my brainstorming phase. It allows for the benefits of a large board, while working in smaller spaces.

Once you have your physical space organized, I would start by determining the main goal or message of your YouTube video. What do you want to _convey_ to your audience? This will help you focus your ideas and ensure that your script stays on track and stays focused on your main message.

Next, consider your _target audience_ and what topics or ideas would be most interesting or relevant to them. This will help you tailor your script to your audience and make sure that it resonates with them.

Once you have a clear idea of your goal and target audience, *now* it's time to start brainstorming potential ideas for your script. Don't be afraid to think outside the box and come up with unique and interesting ideas. Consider using a mind map or brainstorming tool to help visualize your ideas and organize them into a cohesive structure.

I would suggest that you research your topic for at least 2-8 hours (depending on the length of your video) to gather any necessary information or resources that will help you create a more informative and engaging video. This could include statistics, examples, or expert opinions. By including relevant and reliable information in your script, you can make your video more credible and persuasive.

I understand this may seem like a lot of time, but also consider that if this topic or idea takes off and you niche into this within your channel, you will already have to foundation to make a fantastic second or third video for your audience and you will not lose any momentum.

As always, as an added extra, I do suggest getting feedback from others, such as friends or colleagues, to help refine your ideas and make sure they are clear and compelling. Ask for their honest opinions and suggestions, and consider incorporating their feedback into your script.

Finally, never be afraid to experiment and try something new or different. The more unique and interesting your video is, the more likely it is to stand out and engage your audience. Considering how YouTube has recently pushed for older videos in YouTuber's pages to be archived or harder to view, if you do make a video that is not that successful, it will very soon be forgotten by your next great idea.

Researching a "Let's Play" Script

For something more practical, below I have provided a very simple example of how I would go about researching for a video game, *"Let's Play"* video. These questions not only reduce time wasted and keep focus, it can help reduce any anxiety you may have and helps make you feel more confident when filming.

I do want to add that though these types of videos often do not necessarily need a script, but I feel that any script/video can benefit from this stage and therefore have chosen a "Let's Play" video to highlight this assumption.

1. Determine the main goal or purpose of your research:
   - What specific game or genre are you researching?

   - What do you hope to learn or accomplish through your research?

2. Identify the key questions or issues:

- What specific information or insights are you looking for?

- What are the key features or mechanics of the game?

- What is the storyline or plot of the game?

- What are other let's play channels doing in the same genre?

3. Develop a plan or strategy for conducting your research:

- Identify relevant sources of information, such as the game's website, forums, or user reviews, as well as other let's play channels on YouTube.

- Determine how you will access and evaluate this information, such as by reading reviews, watching videos, or participating in discussions.

4. Take careful and detailed notes:

- Include the source of each piece of information

- Note any relevant quotes or statistics

5. Look for patterns, trends, or themes that emerge:

- Analyze the information gathered and identify any trends or patterns in the research

- Identify what other let's play channels are doing that is effective or engaging

6. Review and evaluate your research:

- Ensure that your research is accurate, relevant, and complete

- Identify any gaps or inconsistencies in your information

- Have you addressed all of the key questions or issues that you identified at the beginning of your research?

Script Inspiration

Often you will want to look at other content creators who are within your niche, (please, *please* do this!) however determining if someone is an expert on YouTube can be challenging. There are many factors to consider and there are no definitive criteria for expertise.

Sure, you can look at views and subscription count as a measure of expertise and success but there are a number of factors that determine success. Just because these metrics are high, does not necessarily mean that these channels will provide you the necessary information for effective script writing.

To begin, I would suggest looking at their credentials outside of YouTube. For example, you could look for evidence of their knowledge and expertise in the niche. This could include academic qualifications, certifications, or professional experience in the field. An example of this would be if the person is a YouTube expert, they may have a degree in marketing or communications, or they may have worked in the industry for several years.

Once you have determined this, I would research to see if they have published any articles, books, or other works on the subject. This could indicate that they have in-depth knowledge and expertise on the topic, as well as a commitment to sharing their knowledge with others. For example, a "YouTube expert" may have written a book on YouTube marketing or have a blog that covers YouTube-related topics.

Another factor to consider is the person's contributions or involvement in the community or industry related to the niche. Do they participate in forums, conferences, or other events related to the niche? Do they have a strong social media presence or following in the niche? For example, a YouTube expert may be an active member of a YouTube community forum or may have a large following on social media. This is generally easy to spot if you have watched a few of their videos. Look through their comments and their dialogue and this will often lead to community participation outside the platform.

Now, once you have determined if they are an expert, consider the most important aspect when it comes to using them as script inspiration; their ability to communicate and explain complex concepts or ideas in a clear and concise manner. Can they effectively share their knowledge and expertise with others through their videos and other content on YouTube?

When you are creating your own scripts, you want to be able to convey your expertise (whatever that may be) in a concise and entertaining way. If you want to find inspiration, do your homework so you don't get caught out in the long run if the person you are following turns out to be a charlatan.

CHAPTER 2: THE DIFFERENT TYPES OF SCRIPTS

Choosing the appropriate script

Choosing the appropriate script type for your YouTube video is essential because it can affect the effectiveness and general caliber of the content. Using various script types, each of which serves a different purpose, you can achieve a variety of goals for your video. An educational video's script, for instance, might need to be more instructive, whereas an entertaining video's script might need to be more creative and compelling.

I argue that you can insure that your video is well-organized, understandable, and interesting for your audience by selecting the appropriate script type. It can also help you make sure that your video complies with YouTube's particular guidelines and requirements, such as by adding closed captions for accessibility.

As always, this will depend on your particular niche, but in most cases I would recommend just using something called a *full script*. A full script is a detailed document that outlines every aspect of the video, such as dialogue, narration, and visual elements. This type of script is often used for longer or more complex videos.

If the full script is not necessarily important for your particular niche, another option is an outline script, which is a brief summary of the key points or ideas that will be covered in the video. Outlines provide a high-level overview of the video and may include an introduction, main points, and conclusion. They are useful for organizing the video and making sure all-important points are covered.

Bullet points are another option, which is simply a list of the key points or ideas that will be discussed in the video. This type of script is useful for organizing shorter or simpler videos, or for videos that are more conversational or informal in nature. These are often great for YouTubers who are more free-flowing but still want a very basic structure to their videos, having particular points they need to cover in order to convey the message they intend.

Finally, some youtubers may choose to simply *improvise* their videos without using a written script. This can be a more spontaneous and flexible approach to creating a video, allowing the creator to be more responsive to the needs of the audience. However, it can also be more challenging, as it requires the creator to be prepared and well-informed about the topic of the video. In any case, using a script of some kind can help ensure that the video is well-planned and effective in conveying its intended message. More often than not this can be utilized for most gaming videos and channels which rely on posting daily to stay relevant.

There are pros and cons to each script type and it is important to research which would serve best for your particular niche. Using a full script when not necessary may cause the video to seem ingenuine and stilted, whereas if you forego a script altogether, you may miss particular points which your audience expects from you and you may ultimately hurt your metrics.

I have included some script outlines at the end of this guide; however, the next section will show you a basic structure which may be all you need to begin creating content.

Basic Script Outlines

A script outline is a detailed plan for your script, including the key scenes and the important points that you want to cover. It acts as a roadmap for your script and helps you stay on track as you write.

Here is an example of two very basic outlines for short YouTube videos – Keep in mind, this is very basic, but we will continue to get more in-depth throughout the book, with the most complex being outlined at the end.

These two scripts (one general, one specific) will be the basis for our script building venture.

I. Introduction

- Introduce yourself and the topic of the video

- Provide an overview of the key points or ideas you will cover

II. Body

- Provide background information on the topic

- Present your main points or ideas

- Use examples or visual elements to illustrate your points

III. Conclusion

- Summarize the key points of your video

- Leave the viewer with a strong call to action or next steps

IV. Outtakes (optional)

- Include any bloopers or outtakes that you want to include in the final video

V. Credits (optional)

- Thank any contributors or collaborators who helped with the video

- Include any relevant links or information for the viewer to follow up with you.

Here is an example script for a Let's Play YouTube channel:

I. Introduction

• Hi, everyone! My name is [Your Name] and welcome to my Let's Play channel. Today, I'm going to be playing [Name of the Game].

• [Briefly explain the game and what you will be doing in the video].

II. Body

• [Start playing the game and provide a running commentary of your thoughts and actions as you play].

• [Include any relevant gameplay footage or screen captures].

• [Provide any tips or strategies that you are using as you play].

III. Conclusion

• [Summarize your thoughts on the game and whether you would recommend it to others].

• [Thank the viewer for watching and invite them to subscribe to your channel].

IV. Outtakes (optional)

• [Include any funny or interesting moments from the video].

V. Credits (optional)

• [Thank any contributors or collaborators who helped with the video].

• [Include any relevant links or information for the viewer to follow up with you].

CHAPTER 3: THE THREE SECTIONS

It comes in threes

Scripting the three sections of a YouTube video can be crucial in ensuring that the video is well-structured and engaging. The three main sections of a YouTube video are the *hook,* the *content*, and the *call to action*. Each of these sections serves a specific purpose and, when done correctly, can greatly impact the success of the video.

First, the hook is the first part of the video and its purpose is to grab the viewer's attention and keep them interested. The hook is the first impression that the viewer has of the video and it is important to make it count. A strong and engaging title and thumbnail, as well as an interesting and compelling introduction can be used to achieve this. The hook should provide a clear idea of what the video is about and should set the stage for the rest of the video. This is the section where you want to make sure that the audience is hooked and wants to continue watching.

The content is the main part of the video and it is where the YouTuber <u>presents the information</u>, ideas, or stories that they want to share with the viewer. This section should be well-researched and well-organized, and should be presented in a clear and engaging manner. The content should provide value to the viewer, and should be interesting and informative. This is the part where you want to make sure that your audience is learning something new or getting entertained.

The call to action is the final part of the video and it is where the YouTuber <u>asks the viewer to do something</u>, such as subscribe to their channel, share the video, or visit their website. The call to action should be clear and specific, and should provide a compelling reason for the viewer to take action. This is the part where you want to make sure that your audience is taking some action, whether it is subscribing, sharing or visiting your website.

Understanding these three main sections of a YouTube video can help to ensure that the video is well-structured and engaging, and can increase the chances that the viewer will watch the entire video and take the desired action. Therefore it is vital that your script (whichever type it may be) reflects your understanding of these sections.

Scripting Your First 15 - 20 Seconds

The first 15 - 20 seconds of a YouTube video are the <u>most important</u> because this is the time when the viewer decides whether to continue watching or to click away. During this short time period, the viewer is forming their initial impression of the video, and they are deciding whether it is interesting, engaging, and worth their time.

This means that the first 15 - 20 seconds of a YouTube video are crucial for capturing the viewer's attention and keeping them engaged. If the first 15 – 20 seconds are boring, uninteresting, or confusing, the viewer is likely to click away and move on to something else. On the other hand, if the first 15 – 20 seconds are engaging, interesting, and well-executed, the viewer is more likely to continue watching and to become invested in the video.

When both creating and scripting for this section, in my personal opinion, you, the YouTuber should put <u>40-50%</u> of their effort into the first 15 seconds of their video. This means creating a strong and engaging title and thumbnail, providing a compelling and interesting introduction, and using visuals and other media to grab the viewer's attention and keep them engaged. By doing this, a YouTuber can increase the chances that the viewer will watch their entire video and engage with their content.

Content Section

Writing the content section of a YouTube script is important for a few reasons. First and foremost, it helps you plan and organize your video, ensuring that all of the key points and ideas you want to cover are included in a logical and coherent manner. A well-written script can also help you stay focused and on track as you create your video, avoiding the risk of rambling or getting side-tracked.

In addition, a written script can be helpful for ensuring that your video is clear and easy to understand for your audience. By outlining the key points, you want to make and organizing them in a logical way, you can help your viewers follow along and retain the information you are presenting. A script can also help you ensure that your video has a strong beginning, middle, and end, which can make it more engaging and satisfying for your viewers.

Remember, a written script can be useful for collaborating with other creators or working with a team. It can provide a clear roadmap for everyone involved in the production process, making it easier to coordinate efforts and stay on track. Though, writing the content section of a YouTube script is an important step in the video creation process, helping you create a well-planned, clear, and engaging video for your audience, more often than not I find this section to be quite easy once I have reached a *flow state* in my work.

Try to allow this state to happen, simply scripting one point to the next and conveying your message in it's entirety. Once you have your messaged put forth into the universe, it's time for the audience to pay for your wonderful content.

Call to Action (CTA)

Writing the call to action (CTA) section of a YouTube script is important because it provides an opportunity to encourage your viewers to take a specific action after watching your video. A CTA can be anything from subscribing to your channel, liking the video, commenting on the video, or visiting your website. Whatever action you want your viewers to take, a well-written CTA can be an effective way to encourage them to do so.

There are a few reasons why writing the CTA section of a YouTube script is important. First, it helps you clearly communicate the action you want your viewers to take, making it more likely that they will follow through. By outlining the CTA in your script, you can ensure that it is clearly stated and easy to understand.

A written CTA can help you measure the effectiveness of your video. By including a specific action that you want your viewers to take, you can track the results and see how well your video is performing in terms of engagement and conversion. This can be especially useful if you are using your video to promote a product or service, as you can use the data to optimize your marketing efforts.

Without a written CTA, YouTubers can forget how vital they can be for collaboration and team communication. By outlining the specific action, you want your viewers to take, you can ensure that everyone involved in the production process is on the same page and working towards the same goal.

CHAPTER 4: LANGUAGE

Making a successful and interesting video for your audience on YouTube requires selecting the right language for your script. The target audience, the purpose and content of the script, cultural and regional considerations, and the language in which you feel most at ease and confident when speaking and writing are all significant factors to take into account when making this choice.

Priority one should be given to identifying your target audience and their preferred languages. Are they multilingual or are they more likely to be native speakers of one particular language? Do they prefer formal or *gamer speak*? How will you use language to better connect with your audience? This knowledge can help you decide which language to use for your script because it's crucial to pick a language that your audience will be most likely to comprehend and connect with.

As always, when sitting down to write, think about the script's purpose and content. What words will help you accomplish your goal and connect with your audience and how will this drive channel success?

For instance, using a more formal language might be appropriate if your script is educational and informative, whereas using a more casual language might be more effective if your script is lighthearted and entertaining. It is crucial to pick a language that suits the subject matter you are presenting.

Any cultural or geographic considerations must also be taken into account too. Do you need to be aware of any language-related customs or traditions, or should you take into account any regional differences or dialects? Your script will be inclusive and respectful of your audience if you are aware of these regional and cultural differences.

Something I have only began doing in recent years is adding subtitles or translations in different languages. If you're writing for a multilingual audiences, this can make your script more inclusive and accessible, so by doing this, you can connect with more people and make sure that everyone can understand your script.

My biggest argument for anyone looking to make an authentic script is to utilize language in which you feel confident and at ease when *both* speaking and writing. As a result, you'll be able to deliver your script more effectively and naturally, and your audience will find the language more engaging and authentic. A way I have successfully accomplished this in the past is through the use of *colloquialisms*.

Colloquialisms

The strategic use of slang can be a potent audience-building tool. Content can be made to be more relatable, interesting, and authentic by using colloquial expressions and words, which are frequently used in everyday speech but are not regarded as being a part of the standard language.

It is more crucial than ever to engage audiences on a personal level in the media landscape of today, where they are constantly inundated with content. You can give your writing a more casual, conversational tone by incorporating colloquialisms, which will help you connect with your audience on a deeper level. Use colloquialisms to inject humor and personality into your content, for instance, if you're making a humorous or entertaining YouTube video. This can improve the relatability of your content and strengthen the bond between you and your audience.

Additionally, colloquialisms can be used to add authenticity and genuineness to content. You can produce a tone that is more authentic and natural by using language that is frequently used in everyday speech. This can give the impression that your audience is listening to a real person rather than a script. Your audience will feel more connected to you and your content as a result, helping you to gain their trust and credibility. This is especially crucial in the media environment of today, where authenticity is highly regarded.

It is often used in media and advertisement as a strategy to connect with the audience and in most cases it is effective, so why not use it for your own benefit when creating content and building your brand.

Confidence

Another important aspect is *confidence*. Relaying confidence in your YouTube script is crucial for creating a successful and engaging video for your audience. There are several key strategies that can be employed to convey confidence and authority in your script, including the use of clear and concise language, strong and assertive language, examples and evidence, body language and tone of voice, and practice and rehearsal.

Confidence can also help you to overcome the fear of failure that many beginners experience when starting out. When you're confident in your abilities, you're more likely to take the necessary steps to produce high-quality content, even if it means making mistakes or facing challenges along the way. This can help you to grow and improve as a writer over time.

Without confidence, it is very difficult to communicate your ideas effectively and persuade others to support your vision. When you're confident in your writing, you're more likely to be able to convey your ideas clearly and persuasively, which can be especially important when working with a team or trying to get your ideas approved by a manager or supervisor.

Understanding and gaining confidence in script writing was a turning point in my YouTube journey. My confidence in script would in turn, lead to more confidence on camera and help with both my total views and subscriber count.

The Confidence Steps

First and foremost, it is important to use a clear and concise language in your script. _Avoid using complex or technical language_, and instead focus on using _simple_ and _straightforward_ words and phrases that are easy to understand. This will help you communicate your message clearly and effectively, and will show your audience that you are confident in your knowledge and expertise. Simplifying complex ideas and making them accessible to a wide audience is a sign of true expertise.

Additionally, it is important to use *strong* and *assertive* language in your script. Avoid using weak or passive language, and instead use words and phrases that are strong and assertive. This will help you convey confidence and authority, and will show your audience that you believe in what you are saying. Using assertive language also helps to build a strong and compelling argument, which is important in conveying confidence.

Another key strategy for relaying confidence in your script is to use examples and evidence to support your points. By providing examples and evidence to support your claims, you can show your audience that you are knowledgeable and well-informed. This can help build credibility and trust, and can help you convey confidence in your message. Using evidence to support your claims is a sign of a well-informed expert.

In addition to the words used in your script, your body language and tone of voice can also help convey confidence. For example, when writing your script, remind yourself throughout to utilize confident body language.

This can include things such as standing up straight and making eye contact, using a confident tone of voice, speaking at a steady pace. This helps to reinforce the message of your script and aids in building an emotional connection with the audience. When I first began my journey I had a serious problem with inflections (being Australian and all) and I really had to work on how I presented myself. I made small notes throughout my scripts to remind myself to modulate my speech.

Finally, one of the most essential practices is to rehearse your script before recording it. This will help you become more familiar and comfortable with the content, and will help you deliver your script more confidently and effectively. Practice and rehearsals are essential for building confidence, as it helps to iron out any mistakes, and allows you to get a sense of how you will present the information in a compelling way.

Body Language

As I mentioned earlier, body language can play a big factor in confidence. In everyday life, an essential component of communication is body language, which when applied correctly can significantly increase the effectiveness of a YouTube script.

Creators can add a deeper level of meaning and emotion to their scripts by incorporating body language. This can help them establish a stronger connection with their audience. Additionally, body language can support the script's message, enhancing its impact and ensuring that it is remembered. Body language can also increase the viewer's interest in the video's content. In short, it's crucial to include body language in a YouTube script because it makes the material more relatable, interesting, and memorable for the viewer.

Here is a script for a 10-minute Let's Play YouTube video that includes body language and reminders to be confident and use colloquialisms and be engaging:

- Start by standing up straight and making eye contact with the camera
- Hey everyone! I'm excited to be back with another Let's Play video for you today. (Smile and use a confident

tone of voice)
- In this video, I'm going to be playing (name of game) and I'm really excited to share my experience with you. (Use body language to show enthusiasm, such as gesturing with your hands)
- Now, let's get started! (Use a confident tone and body language to show that you are ready to begin)

As you start playing the game, use colloquialisms and informal language to create a conversational and engaging tone:

- Wow, this game is really challenging! (Laugh and use body language to show frustration, such as scratching your head)
- But I'm not gonna give up! (Use a confident tone and body language to show determination, such as clenching your fist)

Use examples and evidence to support your points and show your knowledge and expertise:

- See, I told you this game was challenging! (Use body language to show frustration, such as shaking your head)
- But I've played it before and I know a few tricks to

Reminders:

- Be confident and use colloquialisms to be engaging
- Use body language to reinforce the message of your script and to build an emotional connection with the audience.
- Use examples and evidence to support your points and show your knowledge and expertise.

CHAPTER 5: PASSION

Do you have it?

If you look at the previous script base, you can see that I tried to incorporate passion in addition to body language to convey my message.

Expressing your enthusiasm for the subject or concept you are discussing in your YouTube script is one of the keys to writing a compelling narrative. Your audience can be inspired and engaged by your passion, which will make your video more compelling and interesting. Here are some ideas to keep in mind if you want to demonstrate your passion in your YouTube script:

Start by determining your areas of passion. What are your passions, hobbies, and interests? What are the subjects or concepts that excite and energize you the most? You can write a script that is genuine and authentic and that reflects your interests and passions by figuring out what your passions are.

Next, express your passion by using language that is forceful and emotive. Avoid using weak or passive language, and instead use words and phrases that are strong and emotive. By doing this, you will be able to make your audience feel the passion and enthusiasm you have for what you are doing.

Use examples and proof to back up your passion. You can demonstrate to your audience that you are knowledgeable and well-informed about your area of interest by giving examples and evidence to support your assertions. As a result, you may gain credibility and trust and be better able to express your enthusiasm.

Your body language and tone of voice, in addition to the words you use in your script, can also help people understand how passionate you are. Employ fervent body language, such as hand gestures and smiles, and a passionate tone of voice, such as speaking more quickly and in a loud, clear voice.

And as I have mentioned in both this book, and my others, before recording your script, *rehearse, rehearse, rehearse!* You'll become more accustomed to and at ease with the material as a result, which will improve the confidence and passion with which you deliver your script.

Using Your Active Voice

Using my active voice was something I initially found challenging when writing scripts. When a sentence or phrase uses the active voice, the action is carried out by the sentence's subject. When a sentence is written in the active voice, the verb in the sentence describes the action being performed, and the subject of the sentence is the one who is doing it.

For example, in the sentence "The cat chased the mouse," the subject is "the cat" and the verb is "chased." The verb "chased" describes the action being performed by the subject, "the cat," who is engaged in chasing.

A sentence or phrase that uses the passive voice, on the other hand, designates the subject of the sentence as the object of the action When a sentence is written in the passive voice, the verb in the sentence describes the action that is being done to the subject and not the subject of the sentence.

For instance, "the mouse" is the subject and "was chased by the cat" is the verb in the sentence "The mouse was chased by the cat." The verb "was chased" describes the action being done to the subject; the subject, "the mouse," is not engaged in the act of chasing.

When writing a script, using active voice can help you write sentences that are clearer, more interesting, and better help you get your point across. Additionally, it can make your script clearer and less likely to cause confusion.

Why My Script Seems Passive

Making an effective and interesting video for your audience requires speaking assertively and with confidence in front of the camera. However, speaking in front of a camera can be nerve-wracking for many people, and it's not unusual for them to sound passive as a result. In this essay, we will look at a number of potential causes for this to happen as well as solutions to help you feel more at ease and productive when speaking in front of a camera.

Nervousness is one of the main causes of people sounding passive when speaking in front of a camera. It can be intimidating to appear in front of a camera, and it's normal to feel self-conscious. This can make someone sound less confident and assertive and cause them to speak in a more passive or subdued tone. Take the time to practice and become familiar with the script, and keep in mind that feeling nervous is normal to help you overcome this.

Lack of preparation is another factor that could cause someone to sound passive when speaking in front of a camera. Lack of preparation or familiarity with the script may make it difficult for someone to speak with assurance and assertiveness. This may make them sound less confident and engaging by causing them to speak more hesitantly or passively. Before speaking in front of the camera, it's crucial to spend the necessary time thoroughly preparing and getting familiar with the script.

Passive voice usage in a script can also make someone appear more passive and less assertive when speaking in front of a camera. When a sentence or phrase uses the passive voice, the subject of the sentence receives the action rather than being the one who performs it. An assertive and confident tone can be communicated by using active voice.

Last but not least, weak or ambiguous wording in a script can make someone appear more passive and less assertive when speaking in front of a camera. Language that is not precise, concrete, or strong is considered weak or vague. When speaking in front of a camera, it's crucial to use strong, precise language to project a self-assured and assertive tone.

As a result, speaking assertively and with confidence in front of the camera is essential for producing an effective and captivating video for your audience. It's common to sound passive in the process, though. One can increase their confidence and effectiveness when speaking in front of a camera by addressing the causes like anxiety, lack of preparation, passive voice use, and the use of flimsy or vague language.

Improving Your Speaking

It's crucial to concentrate on delivering the text authentically rather than simply reading it. Try to slow down and focus on your words in order to speak more effectively and without making mistakes. Given that remembering text is a skill in and of itself, this is similar to what actors do. You can perform better and make fewer mistakes if you concentrate on reading the text aloud.

To accomplish this, it's a good idea to conduct some research and plan your text's flow. When you have a solid plan in place, break it down into key phrases so you can concentrate on speaking the text naturally. To check if you missed any crucial details, record a take and listen to it afterwards. Then carry on until you have a strong text.

If you are having problems, try not to stress too much in the beginning. *Jump cuts* are frequently used by YouTubers to correct errors and keep the flow of their videos. If you're unsure of your ability to perform flawlessly, this is an option. Simply have a few takes and cut them together during the editing phase.

Another choice is to improve your reading skills. News anchors can develop this skill over time by learning it. Being truly proficient in it takes a lot of practice, but once you do, it can enhance your performance and make it simpler to give a polished, controlled vocal performance. To make reading as simple as possible, this calls for specially formatted text that scrolls at the appropriate speed. Even for actors with extensive experience, using a large block of text in front of you will only produce an average performance.

A practical 2023 tip for improving your quality of audio is utilizing Adobe's podcast AI. Simply go to their website and upload your audio (for free) and it will remove background noise and enhance your voice. If you are nervous you can cut your script and recording into blocks, speak quietly into the microphone and the AI will enhance this block of audio into something with a far more polished sound.

Ahhh, the future is here.

CHAPTER 6: HUMOR

Send in the clowns

I have found throughout my time, that in order to engage and entertain viewers, humor is frequently a wise choice for YouTube scripts. When used effectively, humor can make a video more enjoyable and memorable, which can help to boost its popularity and increase the number of views.

Humor can be used in YouTube scripts in a few different ways that are both effective and efficient. First of all, it can be used to add humor and make a video more upbeat and enjoyable. This can help to break up the content and make it easier for viewers to digest, which can be especially useful if the video covers a serious or complicated subject.

Often, I find that humor can be used to give a video a more

intimate and relatable feel. You can make the audience feel more relaxed and at ease by using jokes or humorous anecdotes, which will give them the impression that they are watching a conversation rather than a formal presentation. A video can benefit from the surprise or unexpectedness that humor can bring. You can keep viewers interested in your content by including unexpected jokes or punchlines that will keep them on their toes and engaged.

Humor Tips

YouTube videos that are interesting and entertaining can be produced with the help of humor. It's crucial to use it properly and sensibly, though. In this essay, we'll look at some strategies for effectively incorporating humor into your YouTube script and how to do so tastefully.

First and foremost, it's crucial to begin by coming up with your basic humorous ideas during your brainstorming session. What amusing incidents, stories, or situations could you use in your script? What humorous and relatable situations can your audience identify with? You can write an engaging and entertaining script by coming up with humorous and amusing ideas.

I also find when researching, look for specific GIFs or memes to utilize in your script. Save these away for a specific video or even just for potential future use. Even if you are not a master editor, you can splice these into your content with relative ease.

As I mentioned earlier, I have found it crucial to use colloquialisms and informal language to inject humor and personality into your script in addition to coming up with funny ideas. Remember, colloquialisms are informal expressions or words that are used frequently in daily speech but are not regarded as being a part of the English language. By incorporating colloquialisms into your script, you can establish a more casual and conversational tone, which can enhance your content's personality and humor.

Another thing I like to mention is that it is important to back up your humor with instances and proof. You can demonstrate to your audience that you are knowledgeable and well-informed about the subject by giving examples and proof to back up your jokes or amusing situations. In addition to helping, you deliver your humor more skillfully, this can help you establish credibility and trust.

Again, utilizing your tone of voice and body language to convey humor is another crucial factor to take into account. Your body language and tone of voice, in addition to the words you use in your script, can also help people understand your humor. For instance, you can use amusing body language, like making silly faces or making exaggerated gestures, and an amusing tone of voice, like speaking in a playful or exaggerated way.

A lot of the larger YouTubers practice this, especially in the Hook section of their videos. Look at any of the larger YouTubers at the moment and you will more often than not find exaggerated faces/ gestures in their thumbnails.

Now, not to sound like a broken record but practicing and rehearsing your script is crucial before recording it. This will make the material more familiar to you, which will make it easier for you to deliver your script with more assurance and impact. Please, just do this one for me, I ask so little.

Though this is all good information, it is also important to remember that not all YouTube scripts need to be humorous. Obviously it will depend on the kind of channel you're making. Do not feel compelled to add humor to a video if it will break to tone of the message you are trying to convey.

CHAPTER 7: EDITING

Make or break

It can be difficult to edit a script for a YouTube video, but with the right tools and some practice, it can be a rewarding process that results in a script that appeals to your audience. Following are some suggestions for editing your script.

The first step (*when you're rehearsing*) is to read your script aloud to catch any awkward or unclear phrases. I have found that you will get a sense of how the script sounds when it's spoken from doing this, which can help you make any necessary corrections. As your script should be focused and concise, only including information that is relevant and useful to your audience should be included. Always try to cut out any unnecessary or irrelevant information, unless you are uploading something like a 3 hour stream recording.

Remember, as I mentioned earlier, instead of using complex or technical language that could be perplexing or off-putting, it's important to use simple and straightforward language to make your script more accessible to your audience. Use strong, assertive words and phrases to communicate confidence and authority rather than weak, passive language.

Finally, as is my advice for a lot of the facets of YouTube creation, having another person read and critique your script can be very beneficial. This will assist you in finding any mistakes or errors and offer insightful criticism on how to make your script better. You can see your work with new eyes, spot errors, and ultimately produce a more polished and effective script by looking at it from a different angle.

Revision

There are several steps you can take to edit and maintain the conciseness of a YouTube script. First, carefully read the script and scan it for any extraneous or redundant information. This might take the form of protracted explanations, pointless details, or monotonous language. To make the script shorter, eliminate or omit this information.

Next, look for opportunities to make the script's language more concise and straightforward. This might entail avoiding complex or jargon-filled language in favor of using shorter, simpler words and phrases. The script will become more approachable and understandable as a result.

Utilizing visual components to communicate ideas and information is another strategy. Use graphics, animations, or images to illustrate your points instead of lengthy explanations or descriptions, for instance. The script will become more interesting as a result, and it will also be shorter and more to the point.

Consider working with an editor or a script consultant to review and revise your script. Obviously, his may not be an option for everyone due to budgetary constraints or time/content constraints. An expert editor or consultant can offer insightful criticism and pointers on how to make the script more succinct and clearer. Comparing this to just asking your family and friends to review your work can be a significant improvement (though that can be a great help too).

I encourage you to sit down, without distractions and carefully review the script, looking for opportunities to cut out pointless or redundant information. Have a piece of paper beside you with the message you are trying to convey and ask yourself,

"Is this truly important?"

Editing Software

Seemingly this is becoming less and less important as systems are becoming easier to use, but typically there are a number of factors to account for when selecting editing software that synergizes with your script.

If you are a beginner or intermediate, you do not want to be bogged down with unnecessary functions. Finding software that is user-friendly and simple to understand is first and foremost important. Look for software with an intuitive interface and good tutorials or documentation to help you get up to speed quickly. It's crucial to take into account the features your project will require.

Do you require simple features for video editing, such as trimming and cutting, or do you require more complex tools, such as color grading and compositing? Ascertain that the software you select has the features you require.

Furthermore, make sure the software you select is compatible with the kind of computer you have and the file formats you'll be using. The cost should also be taken into consideration. From open-source software that is available for free to premium paid options, there are many options. Determine your budget range and then look for software that fits it.

Ultimately, to get a sense of which software is most well-liked and respected, it can be useful to do some research and read reviews and suggestions from other users. You can also get recommendations from friends or coworkers who have used video editing software. The ideal editing program for you will ultimately depend on your unique requirements and preferences. Find the software that best suits your needs by taking the time to research and contrast various options.

I would suggest that you experiment. Much like I suggest in the editing book in this YouTube success series, experimentation with different software is quite important for finding ones that 'fit' with your personality and styles. More often than not you can use something basic, but if you want to go to that extra level, I have listed the programs currently used by successful YouTubers.

The Software YouTubers Use

Editing your script is a crucial step in the video creation process for YouTubers. There are several programs and tools that you can use to help you edit your script in order to make sure that it is understandable, succinct, and interesting. We'll go over a few well-liked options for editing your YouTube script in this essay.

Utilizing a word processing program, such as Microsoft Word or Google Docs, is obviously the most common choice for editing your script. These applications provide a variety of features and tools to assist you in editing your script. They are frequently used for writing and editing scripts. You can ensure that your script is polished and professional by using features like spell check, grammar check, and formatting options.

Alternatively specialized scriptwriting software like Final Draft or Celtx is another choice. These programs offer a variety of features and tools to assist you in formatting your script and keeping track of characters and dialogue. They are created specifically for writing and editing scripts. Additionally, you can work together with other authors and distribute your script to others, which makes it simpler for you to get feedback and make adjustments.

Finally, editing and scripts are often done using scripts using video editing tools like Final Cut Pro or Adobe Premiere. Final Cut Pro or Adobe Premiere are commonly used video editing tools like Adobe Premiere or Final Cut Pro. They provide a variety of features and tools that can assist you in editing your script, including trimming and cutting, transitions and effects, and incorporating audio and visual components.

As I mentioned earlier, your personal preferences and the particular requirements of your project will determine the best program to use to edit your YouTube script. You can determine which one suits you and your YouTube script the best by experimenting with a variety of tools and programs. It's critical to select the tool that will make editing simple and enjoyable. With the right program, you can write a script that resonates with your viewers and advances your YouTube career.

Edit or Outsource?

Several aspects, including your budget, your editing abilities, and the particular requirements of your project, will determine whether you should pay someone to edit your YouTube script.

You might want to think about editing your own script if you have a tight budget and feel confident doing so. As a result, you may be able to save money and exert more control over the editing process. However, it might be worthwhile to think about hiring someone to edit your script if you are unsure of your editing abilities or if you have a complicated or large-scale project.

The quality and effectiveness of your YouTube script can be improved by hiring someone to edit it because they can offer their professional expertise and experience. Additionally, they can ensure that your script is polished and prepared for production, saving you time and effort.

But hiring someone to edit your script can be pricey, and you might have to make some compromises along the way. Therefore, it's critical to carefully weigh the advantages and disadvantages of hiring someone to edit your YouTube script before making a choice that best suits your needs and circumstances.

Outsourcing

YouTube scripts can be outsourced in a number of ways. One choice is to look for and hire a freelance script writer using a freelance marketplace like Upwork or Fiverr. You can post a job listing on these sites and get bids from authors who are interested in working on your project. Then, you can check out the writers' ratings, portfolios, and profiles to see which one best suits your requirements.

Utilizing a content writing service like Scripted or Contently is a great choice if you strive for perfection. With the help of these services, you can access a network of qualified writers who can create scripts for your YouTube channel. You can give specific requirements and instructions for your script, and the service will pair you with a writer who is knowledgeable about the pertinent subject and writing style.

A creative company that specializes in writing scripts for YouTube is another option. These companies frequently employ groups of skilled writers who can write original scripts specifically for your channel. They will collaborate with you to comprehend your objectives and target audience before writing a script specifically for you.

Though it can be expensive, hiring a professional writer to write your YouTube scripts is a great way to guarantee that your videos are interesting and well-written. There are numerous options available to assist you in producing high-quality scripts for your YouTube channel, whether you decide to work with a freelance writer, a content writing service, or a creative agency.

CHAPTER 8:

ADDITIONAL SCRIPT

INFORMATION

The Optimal Duration

The type of content you're producing and the preferences of your audience will determine the ideal duration for a YouTube video. YouTube videos typically last for around 15 minutes on average, but they can be as brief as a few seconds or as long as an hour.

The ideal runtime for vlogs, educational content, and other informative videos can be longer because it allows you to go into more detail. For instance, a video that is between 20 and 30 minutes long may be more effective as a tutorial or review.

On the other hand, for entertaining videos like comedy skits or music videos, the ideal runtime might be shorter because it keeps viewers interested and prevents them from tuning out. A comedy skit or music video, for instance, might be more successful if it's under 10 minutes long.

Additionally, because viewers often lose interest in videos that are too long, it's crucial to take their attention span into account. Therefore, it's best to keep your videos as brief and succinct as you can while still giving your audience the information or entertainment they want.

As a result, the ideal length for a YouTube video depends on the kind of content you're producing and the preferences of your audience. In order to hold your audience's interest and give them the information or entertainment they're looking for, it's critical to keep your video brief and interesting.

Visual Elements

I mentioned visual elements briefly before, but it's critical to take into account the visual components that will be used in the script when producing a YouTube video. It's crucial to comprehend how to use these visual components because they are crucial to the message and narrative of the video.

It's crucial to first think about the function of the visual component. What does the visual component hope to achieve? Is it to add more details, make a point clearer, or set a particular tone or ambiance? You can make sure that the visual element is used effectively in the script by understanding its purpose. For instance, if the objective is to convey more information, it may be best to use a static image or animation; however, if the objective is to evoke a particular feeling or atmosphere, a video clip may be more suitable.

Next, it's try to think about the kind of visual component that will be utilized. Will it be an animation, a video clip, or a still image? The right visual element must be chosen for the purpose of the video because each type has advantages and disadvantages of its own. For instance, a static image might work best for giving a precise and in-depth illustration of a point, while a video clip might work better for setting the mood.

The position of the visual component is also very important. Where will the visual component be used in the script? When in the video will it be used—at the start, in the middle, or at the end? You can ensure that the visual element is used at the appropriate time to produce the desired effect by being aware of where it is placed. The use of the visual component, for instance, at the beginning of the video, can be used to draw in viewers and establish the mood for the remainder of the piece.

Finally, think about how long the visual component will be present. When will the visual component appear on the screen? Will there be a brief snippet or will it play for a longer amount of time? It's critical to choose the appropriate duration for the visual element based on the amount of information or detail it needs to convey.

More often than not beginners forget that it's critical to take into account the visual components that will be incorporated into the script when creating a YouTube video; don't make this mistake. To make sure that the visual elements are used effectively to enhance the overall message and plot of the video, it is imperative to take into account the purpose, type, placement, and duration of each visual element. You can produce a visually appealing and potent video that connects with your audience by taking these factors into account.

Common Mistakes

Avoiding common errors that may hurt your video's success is crucial when producing a YouTube video. The most prominent problem I see in new creators is simply not having a clear objective or message for their videos. In my opinion, *this is the most common mistakes that YouTubers make.* The video may feel disjointed and uninteresting without a clear purpose or message, which leads to a lack of focus and direction. It's crucial to know exactly what you want to achieve with your video and to make sure that your script is geared toward achieving that objective. This will enable you to produce a video for your audience that is pertinent, captivating, and interesting.

I have also found that not knowing who the video's target audience is is another common error. If you don't know who your target market is, your script may be too general or broad and fail to connect with them. It's critical to have a firm grasp on who your target audience is and to write your script with their needs and interests in mind. As a result, you will be able to make a video that speaks directly to your viewers and addresses any concerns or interests they may have.

Many YouTubers also make the mistake of not planning out their video in advance. Without adequate planning, the video may be disorganized and contain ideas that are in conflict with one another. In order to write a well-structured and interesting script, it's crucial to take the time to plan out your video, including the key points and ideas that you want to cover. By doing this, you can make sure that your video flows naturally and is simple to understand.

And finally, (something I will mention AGAIN) a lot of YouTubers shoot without properly practicing their script. This might result in awkward or stilted performances, which might turn viewers off. Prior to filming, it's critical to practice your lines and become familiar with the material in order to give a genuine and compelling performance. This will make you feel more at ease and confident while filming, which will improve your ability to engage your audience.

How Long Should I Spend Creating My Script?

When it comes to how much time a YouTuber should spend writing their script, there is no one size fits all solution. The amount of time that is needed will depend on a variety of factors, including the complexity of the topic, the length of the video, and the goals of the video.

In general, as I mentioned earlier, a YouTuber should devote at least a few hours to writing their script. This will give them time to properly research and organize their ideas, and to ensure that the script is well-structured and engaging.

A YouTuber may need to spend more time writing their script if the subject is particularly complex or if the video will be longer. It's a good idea in these circumstances to divide the script-writing process into smaller, more manageable tasks and to allot adequate time to each one.

I have found in the past that the amount of time that a YouTuber should spend creating their script will depend on their specific goals and needs. A YouTuber can make sure they write a high-quality, captivating script that effectively communicates their message to their audience by meticulously planning and organizing their ideas.

However, do not waste time, editing and rewriting a script that is relatively great. Though quality content is a must, you also need to consider how much content you can create. If you are spending all your time scripting, you may not keep up with the demands of your audience and overall your metrics could suffer.

Scripting & Filming

Over the years I have found that because scripting offers a detailed and well-organized plan for the video, it makes it the process of filming just so much easier. A YouTuber can make sure that their video has a distinct beginning, middle, and end, as well as a clear flow of ideas and information, by outlining a script in advance. This makes it simpler to plan the video's layout, including any graphics or other visual components that will be used.

A content creator can also practice their performance in advance thanks to scripting. They can use this before filming to perfect their delivery and make any necessary changes. This can raise the overall caliber of the video and facilitate easier, more effective filming.

Additionally, scripting can assist a YouTuber in avoiding errors and preserving a constant tone and style throughout the video. A YouTuber can prevent losing their focus or forgetting crucial information by having a written script to refer to. This can make the video more coherent and effective, increasing its impact and effectiveness.

CHAPTER 9: THINGS TO CONSIDER

The Perspective of The Viewer

Sometimes I like to sit back and think of the audience. From the perspective of the viewer, scripting improves YouTube videos by ensuring that they are well-structured and simple to follow. A well-written script will have a logical progression of ideas and information, as well as a distinct beginning, middle, and end. This makes it simpler for the viewer to comprehend, interact with, and maintain interest in the video's content.

Besides this, reheating their performance and delivery can rehears and rehears also rehears also rehears also rehears also rehears also rehears also rehears As a result, the video may sound more polished and professional, which makes it more entertaining to watch.

Additionally, scripting can aid in preventing errors and preserving a constant tone and style throughout the video. This can help to maintain the viewer's interest and give the video a sense of coherence and unity.

Overall, scripting improves the viewing experience of a YouTube video by ensuring that it is well-organized, polished, and error-free. A YouTuber can make videos that are more interesting and enjoyable for their viewers by using a script.

A video's experience may suffer if the viewer can tell that the script is weak or nonexistent. A poor script may cause the video to seem disjointed, perplexing, or boring, which may cause the viewer to become disinterested and stop watching. On the other hand, a video may feel haphazard or unplanned, which can also be off-putting, if a viewer can tell that there is no script at all.

A poor script or none at all can, in either situation a bad script or no script at all can detract from the professional and polished appearance of the video, which can speak ill of the video's authorship, as either a bad script can reflect poorly on the video's authorship by By doing this, they risk harming their reputation and losing viewers for future videos.

In order to give their viewers a high-quality, enjoyable experience, YouTubers should carefully plan and script their videos. The structure, interest, and professionalism of the video can be improved by a well-written script, which can also help to increase the YouTuber's reputation and audience.

Increasing View Time

Unfortunately, it's difficult to make a YouTube video that is popular and that viewers will watch through to the end. A You can take a few actions to increase the likelihood that viewers will watch their video through to the end and when I am considering my view time, I like to begin with the script. I ask myself what is important and try to add notes throughout the scripting process, reminding myself of what I can do to engage the audience.

First, it's essential to have a concise and interesting title and thumbnail. The title and thumbnail of a video can help to attract viewers' attention and persuade them to click on it. Make a good first impression because this is how a viewer will perceive your video.

Secondly, creating a strong and engaging introduction is vital. A video's opening seconds are crucial for drawing in viewers and keeping them interested. An effective and interesting introduction can help to establish the tone for the remainder of the video and can maintain the viewer's interest. This can be accomplished by opening with a compelling hook, a provocative question, or a fascinating fact that will capture the audience's interest and compel them to keep watching.

Next, it's crucial to offer useful and engaging content to keep viewers watching your video. Creating informative and interesting content that viewers will find valuable is the best way to keep their attention. This can be accomplished by conducting in-depth research, communicating the information clearly and concisely, and utilizing visuals and other media to enhance the video's content.

Moreover, keeping the video concise and to the point is important. Longer videos may be more challenging to watch, especially if they have a lot of extraneous or irrelevant content. The likelihood that a viewer will watch the entire video can be increased by keeping your video brief and to the point.

Finally, it's critical to develop a compelling and memorable conclusion. An important chance to make an impression on the viewer lasts at the end of a video. A compelling and memorable conclusion can aid in reiterating the video's main points and can entice viewers to share it or watch more of your content. This can be accomplished by restating the key ideas, posing a query, or offering a call to action.

Just remember throughout the process, making a successful YouTube video that viewers will watch through to the end is an art that demands attention to a number of key factors, such as having a clear and engaging title and thumbnail, creating a strong and engaging introduction, providing helpful and interesting content, keeping the video brief and to the point, and creating a strong and memorable conclusion. You can improve your chances of producing a video that will be well-liked by your audience by putting these suggestions into practice.

Utilizing AI to Create a YouTube Script

Using AI to write YouTube scripts is a relatively new approach that has the potential to save time and improve the quality of scripts. AI-powered tools can use natural language processing (NLP) algorithms to analyze existing scripts and generate new scripts that are similar in style and content.

One way to use AI to write YouTube scripts is to input a sample script into the AI tool and provide any relevant instructions or constraints. The AI tool will then use NLP algorithms to analyze the sample script and generate a new script that is similar in style and content. This new script can be used as-is, or it can be edited and revised to meet the specific needs of your YouTube channel.

Another approach is to use AI to generate suggestions for specific elements of your script, such as dialogue or descriptions. You can input a sample script and provide instructions for what you want the AI tool to generate, and it will provide suggestions that you can use in your script. This can be a useful way to get fresh ideas and inspiration for your scripts, and can also save you time by eliminating the need to brainstorm and come up with ideas on your own.

Utilizing AI to write YouTube scripts is a promising approach that can help you save time and improve the quality of your scripts. By using AI-powered tools, you can generate new scripts or get suggestions for specific elements of your script, which can help you create engaging and professional videos for your YouTube channel.

I would however be cautious if you were to use this approach in creating entire scripts. Unofficial news is stating that YouTube has been flagging AI generated scripts throughout 2022 and demonetizing content.

Chapter 9: Example Scripts

Draft 1: Documentary

The below script outlines the content and structure for a YouTube video about the secret life of bees. The video begins with a hook introducing the topic of bees and their importance to the environment and food supply, and includes footage of bees in action. The video is divided into five sections, covering the role of bees in pollination, the history of beekeeping and the evolution of the honeybee, the challenges facing bees and the impact of human activities on their populations, the role of beekeepers and the importance of sustainable beekeeping practices, and the future of bees and what we can do to protect them.

The video ends with a call to action encouraging the viewer to visit the YouTuber's website for more information and to share the video with others to raise awareness about the importance of bees. The video will use a narrator's voiceover, footage of bees, graphics and animation, and music to illustrate and enhance the content.

This script highlights what I feel to be most necessary, including the core elements we spoke about previously.

Title: The Secret Life of Bees

Hook:

• Introduction to the topic of bees and their importance to the environment and our food supply (narrator speaks with enthusiasm and gestures with open hands)

• Show footage of bees buzzing around a hive and collecting nectar from flowers (narrator speaks with wonder and amazement)

• Introduce the narrator and provide a brief overview of the series (narrator smiles and makes eye contact with the camera)

Content:

• 0:00 - 0:15: Hook

• 0:15 - 6:00: Section 1 - The role of bees in pollination and their importance to the environment (narrator speaks with passion and emphasizes key points with hand gestures)

• 6:00 - 12:00: Section 2 - The history of beekeeping and the evolution of the honeybee (narrator speaks with interest and uses hand gestures to illustrate points)

• 12:00 - 18:00: Section 3 - The challenges facing bees and the impact of human activities on their populations (narrator speaks with concern and furrows brow)

• 18:00 - 24:00: Section 4 - The role of beekeepers and the importance of sustainable beekeeping practices (narrator speaks with hope and smiles)

• 24:00 - 30:00: Section 5 - The future of bees and what we can do to protect them (narrator speaks with determination and makes eye contact with the camera)

Call to Action:

• End the video with a call to action encouraging the viewer to visit the YouTuber's website for more information (narrator speaks with excitement and gestures towards the website), and to share the video with friends and family to raise awareness about the importance of bees (narrator speaks with sincerity and makes a heart with their hands).

Audio and Visuals:

• Use a narrator's voiceover to provide information and background on the topic of bees

• Use footage of bees in action, including close-up shots of bees collecting nectar and pollen, and footage of bees inside a hive

• Use graphics and animation to illustrate key points and provide additional information on the topic

• Use music to create a sense of atmosphere and to enhance the mood of the video.

Times:

• 0:00 - 0:15: Hook

• 0:15 - 6:00: Section 1 - The role of bees in pollination and their importance to the environment

• 6:00 - 12:00: Section 2 - The history of beekeeping and the evolution of the honeybee

• 12:00 - 18:00: Section 3 - The challenges facing bees and the impact of human activities on their populations

• 18:00 - 24:00: Section 4 - The role of beekeepers and the importance of sustainable beekeeping practices

• 24:00 - 30:00: Section 5 - The future of bees and what we can do to protect them

• 30:00 - 30:15: Call to action"

Draft 2: Documentary Style

The below script outlines the content and structure for a YouTube docuseries exploring the wonders of the natural world. The series is divided into six sections, each covering a different aspect of the natural world: the introduction, the ocean, the rainforest, the desert, the mountains, and the conclusion. Each section begins with a hook introducing the topic and includes content exploring the unique features and characteristics of the environment, as well as any challenges or threats it faces.

The series also includes call to action encouraging the viewer to subscribe to the youtuber's channel and share the video with others. The series will feature stunning footage of natural landscapes and close-up shots of plants and animals, accompanied by a variety of musical scores to enhance the mood and atmosphere of each section.

Title: "Exploring the Wonders of Our Natural World"

Section 1: introduction (0:00-0:30)

- Hook: have you ever looked up at the night sky and been in awe of the beauty of the stars? (narrator speaks with wonder and gestures upwards) or stood at the edge of the ocean and felt the power of the waves crashing against the shore? (narrator speaks with excitement and gestures towards the ocean) our natural world is filled with wonders that are both breathtaking and mysterious. (narrator speaks with enthusiasm and makes eye contact with the camera)

- Content: in this docuseries, we'll be taking a closer look at some of the most incredible phenomena in the natural world. From the depths of the ocean to the heights of the highest mountains, we'll be exploring the beauty and complexity of the planet we call home. (narrator speaks with excitement and gestures towards a map)
- Audio/visual: this section will feature stunning footage of natural landscapes, accompanied by a sweeping musical score.

Section 2: the ocean (0:30-5:00)

- Hook: the ocean is a vast and complex environment, covering more than 70% of the earth's surface. (narrator speaks with wonder and gestures towards the ocean) it is home to a staggering diversity of life, from the tiniest microorganisms to the largest animals on the planet. (narrator speaks with amazement and gestures towards the ocean)
- Content: in this episode, we'll be diving deep into the ocean to learn about its many mysteries. We'll take a look at the incredible creatures that live there, from the colorful fish of the coral reefs to the mysterious deep sea creatures that we are only just beginning to understand. (narrator speaks with excitement and gestures towards the ocean) we'll also explore the role that the ocean plays in regulating the earth's climate and weather patterns. (narrator speaks with concern and furrows brow)
- Audio/visual: this section will feature stunning

underwater footage of marine life, accompanied by a calming and atmospheric musical score.

Section 3: the rainforest (5:00-10:00)

- Hook: the rainforests of the world are some of the most biodiverse environments on the planet. (narrator speaks with excitement and gestures towards a map) home to millions of different species of plants and animals, they are a vital part of the earth's ecosystem. (narrator speaks with passion and emphasizes key points with hand gestures)
- Content: in this episode, we'll be exploring the incredible world of the rainforest. We'll learn about the unique ecosystem of the rainforest, including the delicate balance between the plants, animals, and microorganisms that live there. (narrator speaks with wonder and gestures towards the rainforest) we'll also take a look at the threats that rainforests face, including deforestation and climate change, and what we can do to help protect these valuable environments. (narrator speaks with concern and furrows brow)
- Audio/visual: this section will feature lush, vibrant footage of the rainforest, accompanied by a lively and energetic musical score.

Section 4: the desert (10:00-15:00)

- Hook: at first glance, the desert may seem like a barren and inhospitable environment. (narrator speaks with skepticism and gestures towards the desert) but look closer, and you'll discover a world of incredible beauty and resilience. (narrator speaks with excitement and gestures towards the desert)
- Content: in this episode, we'll be venturing into the desert to learn about the unique ecosystem that exists there. We'll take a look at the adaptations that plants and animals have developed in order to thrive

in this harsh environment, (narrator speaks with amazement and gestures towards the desert) and we'll also explore the rich cultural history of the desert, including the many indigenous communities that have called it home for thousands of years. (narrator speaks with respect and gestures towards indigenous communities)

- Audio/visual: this section will feature stunning footage of the desert, including sweeping vistas and close-up shots of desert plants and animals. The musical score will be evocative and atmospheric.

Section 5: the mountains (15:00-20:00)

- Hook: the world's highest peaks are some of the most awe-inspiring sights on the planet. (narrator speaks with wonder and gestures towards the mountains) but they are also some of the most treacherous environments, challenging even the most experienced climbers. (narrator speaks with respect and gestures towards climbers)
- Content: in this episode, we'll be heading to the mountains to learn about the unique ecosystem that exists there. We will explore the challenges that plants and animals face in order to survive at high altitudes, (narrator speaks with amazement and gestures towards the mountains) and we'll also take a look at the rich cultural history of the mountains, including the many indigenous communities that have lived there for centuries. (narrator speaks with respect and gestures towards indigenous communities) we'll also hear from experienced climbers as they share their stories and experiences on the world's tallest peaks. (narrator speaks with interest and gestures towards climbers)
- Audio/visual: this section will feature breathtaking footage of the mountains, including aerial shots of

snow-capped peaks and close-up shots of plants and animals that call the mountains home. The musical score will be epic and sweeping.

Section 6: conclusion (20:00-20:30)

- Hook: as we've seen in this docuseries, our natural world is filled with wonders and mysteries that continue to inspire and captivate us.
- Content: in conclusion, we hope that this series has given you a deeper appreciation for the incredible planet we call home. From the depths of the ocean to the heights of the highest mountains, there is always more to discover and learn about the natural world. We hope that you'll join us on future episodes as we continue to explore the wonders of our natural world.
- Audio/visual: this section will feature a montage of highlights from the series, accompanied by a sweeping and uplifting musical score.

Draft 3: Interview/Storybook Style

This script outlines the content and structure for a YouTube video featuring an interview with environmental activist jane doe. The video is divided into five sections, each covering a different aspect of jane's work and experiences: the introduction, jane's early life and career, her major campaigns and accomplishments, her future goals and challenges, and final thoughts and call to action. In the introduction, jane is introduced as an environmental activist with over 30 years of experience, and the video sets the tone with a comfortable and relaxed setting and uplifting background music.

In the second section, jane discusses her background and how she became interested in environmentalism, and in the third section she talks about her major campaigns and accomplishments. The fourth section focuses on jane's vision for the future and the challenges facing the environmental movement, and in the final section jane shares her final thoughts and encourages viewers to get involved and support her work. The video ends with a call to action encouraging viewers to visit jane's website for more information.

Storyboard video script for an interview YouTube channel:

Title: "Interview With Environmental Activist Jane Doe"

Section 1: introduction (0:00-0:15)

- Hook: today we are joined by jane doe, an environmental activist who has been fighting to protect the natural world for over 30 years.
- Content: jane has dedicated her life to advocating for the protection of our planet's precious ecosystems, from the rainforests of the amazon to the polar ice caps. In this interview, we'll be learning about her work, her motivations, and her vision for a sustainable future.
- Audio/visual: this section will feature a shot of jane sitting in a comfortable armchair, surrounded by books and plants. She will be smiling and engaging with the camera, with a warm and friendly demeanor. The background music will be gentle and uplifting.

Section 2: early life and career (0:15-2:00)

- Hook: jane, can you tell us a little bit about your background and how you got involved in environmental activism?
- Content: jane will describe her childhood growing up in a small town in the countryside, where she developed a love for nature and the outdoors. She will talk about how she became interested in environmentalism in college, and how she decided to make it her career. She will also discuss some of the challenges she faced along the way, and how she overcame them.
- Audio/visual: this section will feature footage of jane as a child, playing in fields and forests. Jane will have a nostalgic and emotional expression on her face as she talks about her childhood. The background music will be nostalgic and emotional.

Section 3: major campaigns and accomplishments (2:00-5:00)

- Hook: jane, you have been involved in many high-profile campaigns over the years. Can you tell us about some of your most significant achievements?
- Content: jane will discuss some of the major campaigns she has been involved in, including her work to protect the amazon rainforest and her efforts to raise awareness about climate change. She will talk about the challenges she faced and the successes she has achieved, and she will share some of the lessons she has learned along the way.
- Audio/visual: this section will feature footage of jane speaking at events, attending protests, and interacting with supporters. Jane will have an inspiring and uplifting expression on her face as she talks about her achievements. The background music will be inspiring and uplifting.

Section 4: future goals and challenges (5:00-7:00)

- Hook: looking to the future, what do you see as the biggest challenges facing the environmental movement, and what goals do you hope to achieve?
- Content: jane will discuss her vision for the future of the environmental movement, and the challenges she sees ahead. She will talk about the need to address issues such as climate change and deforestation, and she will share her hopes for a sustainable future for the planet.
- Audio/visual: this section will feature footage of jane looking out at a natural landscape, with a thoughtful and determined expression on her face. The background music will be hopeful and optimistic.

Section 5: final thoughts and call to action (7:00-8:00)

- Hook: before we wrap up, do you have any final thoughts or messages for our viewers?
- Content: jane will share her final thoughts on the importance of protecting the environment, thanking the audience with a smile, before fading to black.

Draft 4: Let's Play!

The final video script titled "Exploring the World of 'Skyrim'" is divided into four sections: introduction, gameplay, mod showcase, and final thoughts. In the introduction, the player sits in front of their computer, ready to play the game and explore the open world. The gameplay section features the player playing the game, providing commentary and interacting with the camera. The mod showcase section showcases some of the mods installed in the game and demonstrates how they work.

The final thoughts section has the player thanking the viewers and providing information on future episodes. The video encourages viewers to like and subscribe, and to follow the player on a social media platform for updates.

"Storyboard video script for a "let's play" YouTube channel

title: "exploring the world of 'Skyrim'"

Section 1: introduction (0:00-0:15)

- Hook: hey guys, welcome back to another episode of "let's play Skyrim"!
- Content: in today's episode, we'll be exploring the vast open world of the game, taking on quests and battling enemies as we go. We'll also be checking out some of the new mods and features that have been added since the last time we played.
- Audio/visual: this section will feature a shot of the player sitting in front of their computer, smiling and looking excited. They will be wearing headphones and have their controller in hand. The background music will be energetic and upbeat.

Section 2: gameplay (0:15-30:00)

- Hook: okay, let's get started!
- Content: the player will begin playing the game, exploring the world and completing quests. They will be narrating their gameplay and providing commentary on their strategies and thoughts as they play. They will also be interacting with the camera and making jokes and puns as they go.
- Audio/visual: this section will feature gameplay footage of the player exploring the game world and battling enemies. The player will be laughing and

smiling as they play, and may occasionally make exaggerated facial expressions or gestures for comedic effect. The background music will be energetic and suspenseful.

Section 3: mod showcase (30:00-45:00)

- Hook: one of the things i love about Skyrim is the huge modding community. Let's take a look at some of the cool mods we've added to the game!
- Content: the player will showcase some of the mods they have installed in the game, demonstrating how they work and explaining what they add to the gameplay experience.
- Audio/visual: this section will feature footage of the player showcasing the mods, with a excited and enthusiastic expression on their face. The background music will be energetic and upbeat.

Section 4: final thoughts (45:00-50:00)

- Hook: well, that's all the time we have for today. What did you guys think of the episode?
- Content: the player will wrap up the episode by thanking the viewers for watching and encouraging them to leave comments and suggestions for future episodes. They will also provide information on where to find them online and what they have planned for future episodes.
- Audio/visual: this section will feature a shot of the player looking directly at the camera, with a friendly and sincere expression on their face. The background music will be gentle and uplifting.
- Call to action: don't forget to like and subscribe if you enjoyed the episode, and follow us on [social media platform] for updates on future episodes. Thanks for watching, and we'll see you in the next one! "

CONCLUSION

In conclusion, writing a YouTube script is a crucial stage in the production of videos. It facilitates thought organization and guarantees that your video transitions seamlessly from one segment to the next. You can create captivating and effective YouTube scripts that will captivate your audience and keep them coming back for more by using the advice and strategies provided in this book.

Having a strong script will help you elevate your content and stand out in a crowded online landscape, regardless of your level of experience as a creator or your level of familiarity with the world of video production. Therefore, it is wise to spend some time writing and editing your script before pressing the record button. With some practice and perseverance, you'll be well on your way to producing YouTube videos that are both entertaining and informative, reaching your target audience and creating sustainable success.

Author's Note

As always, I want to express my sincere gratitude
to each and every one of my readers for taking
the time to interact with my writing.

Your encouragement and interest in my writing are

greatly appreciated, and I am motivated to keep writing because of your continued engagement. I am appreciative of the chance to communicate with you and hope that my writing has been both educational and enjoyable.

Ben.

Printed in Great Britain
by Amazon

26131840R00046